MONUMENTAL AMERICA

Table of Contents

White House

What would it be like to live here?

The White House is the President's home.

Inside there are:

132 rooms,

35 bathrooms,

a tennis court,

a swimming pool,

a jogging track,

a movie theatre, and

a bowling alley.

Wow, what a house!

Washington Monument

Compare this monument to the Lincoln Memorial.

At 6 feet 3 inches tall, George Washington was taller than most people. The Washington Monument is taller than most monuments. It is even taller than the nation's **capitol**. There are 896 steps from bottom to top. That's tall.

Jefferson Memorial

What do you like best about this building?

Thomas Jefferson's favorite building was the Pantheon in Rome. The Jefferson **Memorial** was built in the same shape. It has a huge **dome** and a statue of Thomas Jefferson inside.

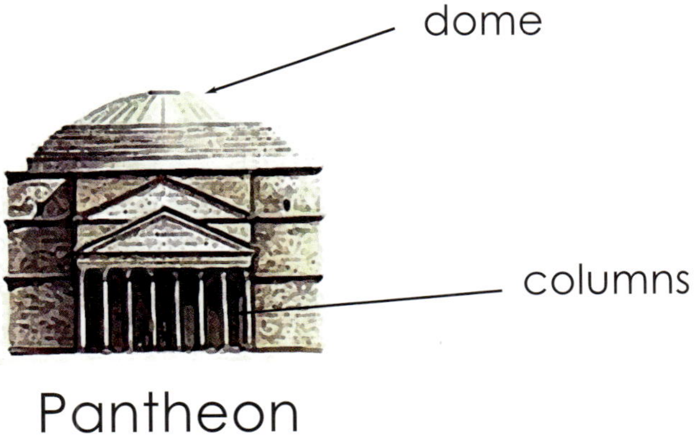

Pantheon

Vietnam Veterans

How would it feel to stand beside this wall?

This memorial is made up of two walls. Each is more than 246 feet long. Many Americans served in the Vietnam War. The names of the American soldiers who died there are shown on the black granite walls. There are 58,325 names listed.

Tomb of the Unknowns

What do you think this soldier is thinking?

This monument reminds us of the unidentified American soldiers who fought and died for our country. It is in Arlington National Cemetery in the state of Virginia. As a symbol of <u>respect</u>, the tomb is always guarded by a soldier.

World War II

Discuss the design of this memorial.

World War II was the world's biggest war. 16 million Americans fought, and over 400,000 died. In 2004 the WWII Memorial, long overdue, was dedicated to all who served in the Big War. Because of their sacrifice, we are free today. We proudly salute them.

Lady Liberty

What does the Statue of Liberty mean to you?

My Country 'Tis of Thee

My country 'tis of thee,
Sweet land of liberty,
Of thee I sing.
Land where my
fathers died,
Land of the Pilgrim's pride,
From every mountain side,
Let freedom ring.

Glossary

capitol: the building in Washington D.C. where the government is based

dome: a roof shaped like half of a sphere

honor: show gratitude and respect

memorial: an object built to help us remember a person or event

Index